P... ...rated by ...

BIBLE
Detective

LION
CHILDREN'S

Noah, the good herdsman

According to the Bible, God sent a flood because the world had grown wicked. This picture, based on finds from ancient Mesopotamia, shows Noah as a decent herdsman trying to take care of himself and his family.

The people around him are less kind: drunkenness, bullying, and violence are common.

People cross the river in skin boats, called guffas. Find one with animals in.

Men and women use long straws to share a vat of beer. Can you see them?

These soldiers wear leather helmets and woollen cloaks. Find 8.

In some places tar oozes to the surface. Spot Noah smearing it on a guffa to make it watertight.

Wild animals threaten flocks. Lions are among the most feared. Spot the male lion.

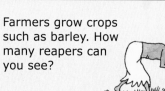

Farmers grow crops such as barley. How many reapers can you see?

Women grind grain at home with a very simple mill. Find Noah's wife at work.

Bronze-tipped weapons are the sharpest available. Spot an axe.

Only the wealthy have chariots. Spot a charioteer being unkind to the poor.

People use bows and arrows to hunt and kill deer. Find 3 hunters.

Boys splash and swim with floats made of animal skin. Spot a boy fishing.

The river is the main source of water. Find 2 of Noah's daughters-in-law doing laundry.

Noah's wife needs water to make bread. Spot her daughter-in-law bringing water from the river.

Olive trees are carefully tended, as the fruits are rich in delicious oil. Spot an olive press.

The Royal Game of Ur is a race game with a special game board. Find a game being played.

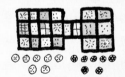

People keep goats, which are not fussy eaters and thrive on very little. Find Noah's 3 sons driving his flock.

Sheep graze on meadows by the river. It floods often. Find 5 riverside pools.

1

Abraham's nomadic encampment

The story of the people of Israel, later known as the Jews, really begins with Abraham. According to the Bible, he believed God was telling him to leave the city life of Mesopotamia to make a new home in the land of Canaan.

He went with all of his household and lived as a nomad, leading his flocks to wherever there was pasture.

Wells had to be dug for precious water. Spot 2 women quarrelling over a well.

Women spun and wove the wool from their sheep. Spot a spinner and a weaver.

Stones were arranged within each campfire for cooking on. Find bread being baked on a stone.

It was a tradition to offer food and shelter to strangers. Find 3 people in foreign dress.

Goats would feed in rough pasture. Spot one stuck in a thorn bush.

Look for a trader with his caravan. How many donkeys can you see in the caravan?

An altar like this was a place to burn offerings as a sacrifice to God. Find one in a grove of trees.

Spot a boy carrying his little brother.

Goatskin could be stitched into a wine container. Find 2 containers.

Men wore brightly patterned kilts. Can you see 5 kilts in this pattern?

Nomads traded with local Canaanites for goods they could not produce themselves, such as grain. Spot the Canaanite trading cart.

Look for a man milking a goat.

Find a servant girl being told off by her mistress.

Canaan was not a wilderness: the Canaanites lived there in walled cities. Can you see one?

Spot a baby cradled in a hammock – a portable cradle.

Find 2 young men going hunting with a bow and arrow.

Find 2 girls: one playing the harp and one singing.

Slaves in Egypt

Bricks were made from mud packed into a mould and turned out. Find 5 men using a brick mould.

A device called a shaduf lifted water from the river into irrigation channels. Spot a shaduf.

The mud for bricks had to be mixed with chopped straw. Find 3 men carrying bundles of uncut straw.

Slave-drivers were cruel. Spot 2 whipping a slave.

Waterfowl are hunted. Spot 4 ducks.

Abraham's son Isaac had two sons, Jacob and Esau. Jacob in turn had 12 sons, but his favourite was Joseph. Jealousy led the older brothers to sell Joseph as a slave. In Egypt, he rose to a high rank and, in a time of famine, forgave his family and invited them to leave Canaan for Egypt.

The land was fertile and, with irrigation, produced good crops. However, the time came when a new pharaoh made the people his slaves. They toiled in the brickfields making mud bricks for the pharaoh's grand building projects.

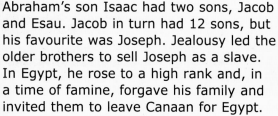

Papyrus reeds had many uses. Find men gathering reeds.

Find a woman coiling a basket from reeds.

Roast lamb was meat for a feast. Spot a boy trying to catch a lamb.

Melons were a much-loved crop. Spot 2 children sharing a melon.

Extra grain from good harvests was stored in silos. Find 4.

Cattle could grow fat on the lush riverside grass. Find 9.

A wealthy person might travel by barge. Spot a barge with the princess on.

The Egyptians had great respect for cats. Find 5.

Scribes kept a record of the amount of grain collected and stored. Find 2 at work.

Frogs can be a nuisance for those who live by the river. Spot 9.

Wild herbs, though sometimes bitter, were collected as food. Spot 3 girls foraging.

A high-ranking official would travel by chariot. How many guards are there making sure the way ahead is clear?

Tambourines were a popular musical instrument. Find 4 girls dancing.

A royal prince goes hunting. How many lions are fleeing?

3

Moses, the Law, and the tabernacle

Moses was one of the people of Israel but adopted at birth by an Egyptian princess. As a grown man he took up the cause of his own people and led them out of slavery in Egypt back to the land of Canaan, which they believed God had promised them since the time of Abraham. They spent years in the Sinai wilderness between Egypt and Canaan. There, God gave Moses the Law, including the ten commandments, and instructions on how to build a place of worship: the tabernacle.

The ten commandments were inscribed on stone tablets and kept in the ark of the covenant. Can you find it?

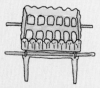

Find the lamp stand inside the tabernacle. How many branches does it have?

Find 2 priests laying 12 loaves on a table.

The high priest wears a breastplate with 12 stones – one for each of the great families of Israel. Can you see him?

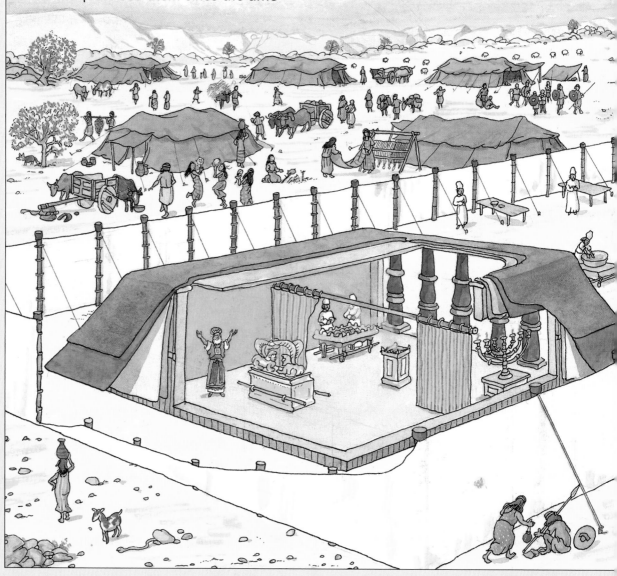

Priests wear a white tunic and turban. Find 11.

Priests washed in a bronze basin before conducting worship. Can you spot it?

Spot a snake.

Incense was burned on a small altar. Can you spot it?

Find the large altar for burning offerings.

Spot 6 ox carts.

How many pillars are at the front of the tabernacle?

Find a child carrying his pet lamb on his shoulders.

Find 2 women folding a length of cloth together.

Spot a flock of quails.

Find 3 men fighting.

Find 2 priests with silver trumpets, which were sounded to summon the people.

Spot 2 men carrying a bunch of grapes on a pole.

Find 3 women carrying water pots.

4

Farming the land

Moses did not live to enter Canaan. He passed the leadership to a bold young warrior named Joshua. He led the people of Israel into the land of Canaan and enabled them to settle there. For the first time, the people became settled farmers in a land they claimed as their own.

The harvesting team would cut barley with a sickle. Spot the field being cut.

Reapers gathered the barley into sheaves. Find 2.

The threshing sledge was set with stones to cut the stalks and loosen the grain. Spot 3 children riding on one.

A shallow basket was used to winnow the threshed barley. This let the chaff blow away, leaving the grain. Find a woman winnowing.

Pruning knives like this were used to trim and tidy grape vines to get a good crop. Spot 2 vine-tenders.

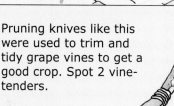

Find 2 children picking peas.

Rock hyraxes sometimes raided orchards. Spot 2.

Flax stalks were laid out in the dew and rain on roofs, so the stalk would rot away and leave the linen fibres. Spot a woman laying out flax.

Spot a woman watering a melon patch.

Figs could be dried in the sun so they would keep. Spot a woman laying out figs.

Water must be drawn from a well. Spot a woman who has dropped her pot.

Bread was baked in beehive-shaped ovens. Find a boy trying to run off with a loaf!

The people feared raiders, such as the camel-riding Midianites. Find 3 Midianite spies.

Find a tired farm worker having a rest in the shade.

Hoeing down weeds leaves vegetables room to grow. Find 3 hoes.

Find a goat in an olive tree.

Thieves might steal grapes. Spot 3 watchtowers from which the 3 vineyards would be guarded.

5

A battle against the Philistines

Goliath was well equipped with iron-tipped weapons. Spot his sword, spear, and javelin.

Spot Goliath's feather-trimmed Philistine helmet.

David came to the battlefield bringing food from home for his brothers. Find 3 baskets of food.

Philistines wore heavy bronze body armour. Spot a soldier sitting down.

The people of Israel faced many enemies as they tried to settle in Canaan. A warrior named David finally defeated them all, and he became the people's king. His most famous battle was when he was just a shepherd boy and he defeated Goliath, the champion of the Philistines.

David learned to use a sling against wild animals. Find him flinging a stone with it.

Spot Goliath's shield-bearer running for his life.

The Philistines had the technology to sharpen iron, so their weapons were strong. Find a blacksmith in the Philistine camp.

How many vultures are circling the battlefield?

Spot King Saul on a throne like this one.

The king had messengers to relay news of the battle. Find the men with horn trumpets.

Count the Philistine war chariots.

Count the Philistine supply carts.

A priest might be asked to advise on tactics. Spot a priest in the Israelite camp.

Find soldiers roasting a lamb.

King Saul offered David his armour for the fight. Where is the royal suit of armour?

David spent some time as a musician to King Saul. Find another musician playing a harp.

Spot a stream running between the enemy camps.

Find soldiers roasting a lamb.

King Solomon's Jerusalem

Animals were slaughtered and burned as sacrifices. Spot an altar where sacrifices were burned.

The priests were required to wash before performing the rituals. Spot a huge bronze water tank.

Two bronze columns stood by the Temple entrance. They have names: spot Jachin on the left and Boaz on the right.

Many Temple ceremonies included music. Find a band of musicians practising their instruments.

David was a warrior whose victories made his kingdom secure. His son Solomon enjoyed the benefits of this power and he became hugely wealthy. He transformed David's capital city, Jerusalem, from a fortress to great city with a gleaming Temple as well as an elaborate palace.

Find 10 awnings providing rooftop shade.

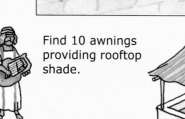

How many Temple storerooms can you see?

Find 5 pomegranate trees.

Can you spot 10 washbasin carts like this one?

The Queen of Sheba came from many miles to the south to see if Solomon was as wise as was claimed. Can you see her?

From where is King Solomon watching?

Solomon had 10 gold lamp stands made for the Temple. How many can you see?

The stone tablets on which the ten commandments were written were at the heart of the people's promise to God. They were kept in a gold box – the ark of the covenant. Can you see it?

The arrival of a queen would demand a feast. Spot cooks roasting a calf.

Solomon controlled trade through his kingdom and imported many exotic things. Find 3 baboons.

Solomon had many wives and children. Spot palace children playing in an outdoor pool.

Solomon invested in horses and chariots, which represented status as well as military might. Spot a group of horse-drawn chariots.

Solomon imported cedar from Tyre – still a port in modern-day Lebanon. Find a wagon loaded with cedar trunks.

An Assyrian attack

The Assyrian army had regiments of slingers. Find a group of them.

Battering rams were used to break down gates and walls. Spot 2.

Defenders threw blazing torches down at the enemy attackers. Find 4 torches.

Large shields of packed straw protected archers. Find 6 shields.

When Solomon died, there was a problem over the succession. In the end the kingdom split: Israel to the north and Judah to the south. Neither kingdom was particularly powerful. To the north, the Assyrians had a fearsome army… and ambitions of ruling a vast empire.

When they attacked, Israel was defeated and the people scattered. Judah stayed free, although some of its cities, such as Lachish, fell to the enemy.

Defeated fighters might be executed. Find one pleading for mercy.

Carts were used to take booty and prisoners away. Spot 2 carts.

Spot the emperor on his throne.

Women and children were taken captive. Spot a woman carrying a child.

The Assyrian emperor demanded gold and silver from the king of nearby Jerusalem. Spot laden camels bringing this tribute.

War chariots were useful in pitched battles more than in sieges. Spot a chariot being repaired.

Armies needed lots to eat. Find 3 children gathering figs for soldiers.

War splits families. Spot 2 children who are holding hands as they look for their parents.

Defenders used spears to wound attackers. Find 2 Assyrians who are falling off ladders.

In a war, there is no time for farming. Find 2 sheep and a goat looking for something to eat.

Swords were used for hand-to-hand fighting. Spot a pair of people in a sword fight.

Even in the military camp, servants had to fan the emperor. Find 2 people with fans rushing to take their turn.

Soldiers who scaled the walls on ladders risked their lives. Find 5 ladders.

8

2 Kings 24–25; Daniel 1–3 / 604–537BCE

Exiles in Babylon

Dried dates were a handy snack. Find a child eating some.

Spot this design on blue tiles on the Ishtar gate.

Marduk was a Babylonian god. Spot his statue.

Spot 3 different types of musical instruments being used in the procession.

Military success meant many prisoners were taken as slaves. Find 3 slaves tending potted trees.

The southern kingdom of Judah did not fall completely to the Assyrians. It stayed independent for more than a hundred years. Then the Babylonians defeated the Assyrians and their empire. They also took Judah. Many of the people of Judah were taken to live as exiles in Babylon. There they became known as the Jews.

Babylon was famous for its "hanging gardens". Spot a boat transporting a large tree.

Find 4 boys fishing from coracles.

Lion hunting was popular with the rich and powerful. Spot a caged lion.

9

Find a horse.

Spot a pickpocket in the crowd.

Find a guard with a mastiff.

Daytime temperatures can soar in Babylon. Spot 11 parasols.

Not everyone wanted to bow down to the Babylonian god. Find 3 Jews refusing.

The Jews tried to keep their customs in Babylon. They met as a "synagogue" on a riverbank under willow trees. Spot a group of Jews going out of the city by boat.

Babylon's stepped temple tower, or ziggurat, was dedicated to Marduk. Can you see it?

Spot a scribe recording the event on a wax tablet.

Babylon is a riverside city. Find a heron.

Elephants from Africa were a real status symbol. Spot 2.

Find 4 archers guarding the procession.

A census in Bethlehem

The Bible story of the birth of Jesus is set in Bethlehem, at the time when the Roman emperor Caesar Augustus had ordered a census throughout the lands he ruled. Everyone had to go to their home town, and for this reason Joseph went with Mary to the town of Bethlehem – also famous as the birthplace of King David.

With many people away from home, Bethlehem was full. Find a couple pleading for a room.

A shelter on the roof could provide space for visitors. Can you see 3?

Find an ox in a stable.

Donkeys carried loads on long journeys. Find 2.

The local ruler King Herod was paranoid about rivals. Spot 2 of his spies exchanging a secret note.

Freedom fighters were always looking for a way to overthrow Roman rule. Find such a man with a sword.

Spot 2 women carrying pots on their heads.

Spot a servant loading hay into a manger.

People from Samaria were not welcome in Jewish towns. Spot a rabbi telling some to find somewhere else to stay.

A woman is being robbed of her money. Can you see the culprit?

How many doves can you see?

People who helped the Romans were disliked as collaborators. Find the local tax collector taking the census for the emperor.

Newborn babies are swaddled to keep them snug. Spot a young mother with her child.

Many people who made the journey to their home town would stay with relatives. Spot a family reunion.

Find a goat eating a shoe.

People obviously from distant lands were rarely seen in Bethlehem. Can you spot an African visitor?

Roman soldiers would police the census. Find 5.

Spot a shepherd boy trying to catch a runaway sheep.

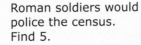

10

A schoolboy in Nazareth

Spot a rabbi teaching in the school room.

Find a woman playing a harp.

Most carpenters' tools of Jesus' day were like those used now. Spot the bow drill, which is less often seen.

The menorah, or seven-branched lamp stand, is a reminder of the one first made for the tabernacle (page 4). Find one in the synagogue.

Jesus grew up in Nazareth. He would have learned to read and write like the other boys at the synagogue school. He would have learned a trade from Joseph.

The scriptures are written on scrolls and kept in a cupboard called the ark. Find the ark.

Very religious people wore extra-long tassels on their prayer shawl. Spot 3 men standing praying in the street.

Spot a mother drawing water from the well.

Hoops, balls, and skittles have been children's toys for centuries. Find 2 children playing.

Spot 3 people riding donkeys.

Spot a shepherd carrying a lamb on his shoulders.

Find 2 women brushing out their houses.

Spot a sower scattering seed from a basket.

Spot village girls making a canopy for the bride and groom to sit under on their wedding day.

In Jesus' day, people who were too unwell to work often had to beg. Find 3 beggars with begging bowls.

Find an old man watching the world go by from his rooftop.

Find 2 workers drinking from a wineskin as they take a break.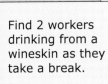

A flock of sheep is running amok. How many sheep are in the street?

Spot a donkey driving an olive mill.

How many oxen are eating from a manger?

A fishing town on Lake Galilee

Find a queue of people waiting to pay the tax collector.

Spot Jesus preaching.

How many cattle are drinking by the lake?

Because Jesus could heal people, those who were unwell were eager to see him. Find 5 people with crutches.

When Jesus became a preacher, he left his home in Nazareth and went to the lakeside town of Capernaum. He made friends with some of the men who fished on Lake Galilee and asked four of them to be his first disciples.

They helped Jesus preach his message about what it meant to live as friends of God.

Fish were caught in a net hung between two boats. Spot a pair of boats.

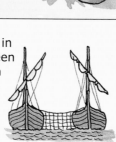

Find 6 baskets of fish.

Spot a woman trying to light her lamp from another's.

Spot 2 Roman soldiers patrolling the lakeside.

Find a man chasing a runaway donkey.

Simple board games might be drawn in the sand. Find 2 boys playing.

Can you find these market traders?

Basket seller

Vegetable seller

Cloth seller

Olive oil seller

Sandal seller

Find a man driving a team of oxen to make a straight furrow.

Spot a woman weaving at her loom.

A Roman soldier could ask anyone to carry their pack a Roman mile. Spot a man bent under the load.

How many children are swimming in the lake?

The Temple courtyard

Jesus became famous among his people – for his preaching and for his healing. Some people even wanted him to become king. However, Jesus often clashed with the religious leaders who wanted him out of the way for good. When he went to the Temple in Jerusalem for a festival, there was almost bound to be a showdown.

Festival-goers needed to change regular money for Temple coins so they could make their offering. Find a money changer.

Live animals were on sale for Temple sacrifices. Find 8 lambs.

Find a pigeon cage.

Romans were not allowed to enter the Temple but still guarded it to ensure order was kept. Spot 6.

Find the high priest with his jewelled breastplate.

Spot a priest directing the musicians.

Find a pickpocket stealing money from a frazzled pilgrim.

Religious teachers – rabbis – wear prayer shawls over their heads. Find one reading a scroll.

One of Jesus' followers, Judas Iscariot, betrayed Jesus to his enemies. Find Judas talking to some rabbis.

Spot someone chasing a dog that should NOT have got into the courtyard.

Spot a poor woman counting out coins to give as an offering

The Temple of Jesus' day was newly designed and still being finished. Spot a crane.

Spot the Roman garrison, the Antonia fortress, that overlooked the Temple courtyard.

Jesus was dismayed at the way the Temple courtyard had been turned into a marketplace. Spot him pushing over a table and telling the cheating traders to go.

Spot musicians playing a psalm of worship.

Spot the Roman governor, Pontius Pilate.

Find the roof of the Temple sanctuary, which was the part of the Temple pilgrims could first see as they approached the city.

The death of Jesus

Two criminals were crucified at the same time as Jesus. Spot their bodies wrapped in cloth.

Bodies were buried as soon as possible. Spot the friends of Jesus carrying his body away.

Bodies were laid in stone tombs to rot. Spot one with a round stone door.

Find 3 ravens.

Spot 6 olive trees near the site.

When Jesus was betrayed by one of his friends, his powerful enemies were able to arrest him. They persuaded the Roman governor, Pontius Pilate, that Jesus was a danger to Roman law and order – someone who might lead the people to rebel and make Jesus king. Pilate was not convinced but he gave the order for Jesus to be crucified.

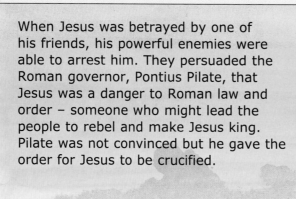

Jesus was betrayed by Judas Iscariot, who was overcome with remorse. Can you find him?

Spot the Roman governor, Pontius Pilate.

Armed rebellion was something the Romans feared. Find a group of freedom fighters.

Jesus asked his friend John to look after his mother, Mary. Can you find them?

Spot someone planning mischief with his slingshot.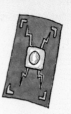

Find 9 of these shields.

Spot 2 ladders.

Find the top of the Temple building.

Spot a man raking the sand.

Crucifixion involved nailing the victim to a cross through the heel and arm. Find 2 mallets.

Jesus was bullied by his executioners. Find the crown of thorns they rammed on his head.

Soldiers gambled for Jesus' clothes rather than tear them. Find them playing a dice game.

Find 2 stray dogs.

The victim's crime was written on a notice they carried to their execution so it could be nailed to the cross. Spot 3.

IESVS NAZARENVS REX IVDAEORVM

Spot 2 beggars.

Peter preaches about Jesus

Find Peter. Once a fisherman in Galilee, he had been a close friend of Jesus for 3 years and believed God helped him speak confidently.

Spot two guards.

Spot the lady of the house.

Find 3 oil lamps.

Spot a mosaic floor.

Jesus' friends laid him in a tomb. They thought that was the end of him and his message. Three days later, however, they claimed they had seen him alive, and that he had told them to spread his message. Strengthened by God, they spoke boldly – first to people in Jerusalem and then in places further away.

Jesus had identified Simon Peter as the rock on which his church would be built. Here he is preaching to the household of a Roman centurion.

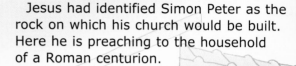

Spot 2 servants bringing plates of food.

Cornelius was a Roman centurion who invited Peter to preach about Jesus. Find Cornelius dressed in ordinary clothing.

Find a donkey laden with goods.

15

Spot a slave taking notes on Peter's speech.

Find a kitchen worker listening in.

Spot 6 children listening.

Spot a slave with garden clippers.

Find 2 sparrows.

Find 2 cats.

Spot 3 footstools.

Spot a mouse.

Find an iris in a vase.

Cornelius was a "God-fearer" before he met Peter and probably attended the synagogue. Spot a rabbi.

Spot scrolls in a cupboard.

Find a child's ball.

Preaching in Corinth

Priscilla and Aquila were friends of Paul, fellow believers and fellow tent-makers. Can you see them?

How many soldiers are inspecting the tent?

Greek cities often had many statues to the gods. How many niches with statues can you see?

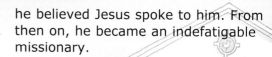

Among the people who spread the news about Jesus was a man named Paul. A devout Jew, he had violently opposed the believers at first. Then, even as he went on a journey to hunt them down, he had a conversion experience in which he believed Jesus spoke to him. From then on, he became an indefatigable missionary.

Find these 3 amphorae.

Paul advised the Christians in Corinth not to have lawsuits against each other. Spot 2 businessmen arguing.

Paul's friends Silas and Timothy met up with him in Corinth. Can you see them?

Paul preached that as Jesus had risen from the dead, believers need not fear death. Find a funeral procession.

Spot a rich woman being carried through the streets in one of these.

Purple cloth was a luxury item. Spot the shop where it is sold.

Spot a storyteller surrounded by children.

Find the fruit stall.

Find the bread stall.

Spot a dog scavenging bones.

Paul wrote letters to places he had visited and sent messengers to deliver them. Find a messenger racing through the marketplace.

Spot this carving of an emperor.

Christians in the Roman world wondered if it was right to eat meat that had been offered to other gods. Find the butcher's shop.

The port of Caesarea

Paul's preaching was not always popular, as people felt their old beliefs being challenged. In the end, it was the religious leaders in Jerusalem whom he had once supported who hated him the most. When they put him on trial, he exercised his right as a Roman citizen to appeal to the emperor. This provided him with the chance to go to Rome and visit the believers there – albeit under arrest!

Spot Paul leaving for Rome.

The governor Festus approved Paul's going to the emperor's court. Spot him watching the departure.

Paul travelled on a merchant ship. How many people are carrying sacks of grain?

Find 2 dockside cranes.

Find the other prisoners being boarded onto the same ship as Paul.

Can you see some local believers waving Paul a fond farewell?

Spot a warship with many oars worked by galley slaves.

Amphorae were used for transporting goods such as wine, oil, and fruit. Find a wagon loaded with them.

Roman glassware was a luxury item. Spot a man packing bottles into a barrel filled with straw.

Spot a seagull swooping on someone's lunch.

Passengers on boats often had to take their own supplies. Find a woman packing a hamper.

Find 2 men drinking wine who look like they've stolen it from a cart.

Giant steering oars in the stern were used to steer sailing boats. Spot one being refitted.

Anchors secure a boat in the water. Find a sailor lifting one up.

Spot some children helping themselves to watermelons.

Wicker baskets and bags would commonly be used for luggage. Find a family struggling with their luggage.

Spot some workmen mixing concrete for harbour repairs.

Spot some priests frowning at seeing Paul being allowed to appeal their judgment.

1 Noah, the good herdsman

The answers are given in this order: start with the picture in the top left. Then go round counterclockwise.

Guffa with animals in 1
A vat of beer 2
Soldiers wearing leather helmets and woollen cloaks 3 4
  5 6 7 8 9 10
Noah 11
Male lion 12
Reapers 13 14 15 16 17
Noah's wife 18

An axe 19
Noah's sons 20 21 22
Riverside pools 23 24 25 26 27
Royal Game of Ur 28
Olive press 29
Noah's daughter-in-law carrying water 30
Noah's daughters-in-law doing laundry 31 32
Boy fishing 33

Hunters 34 35 36
Unkind charioteer 37
Fox 38

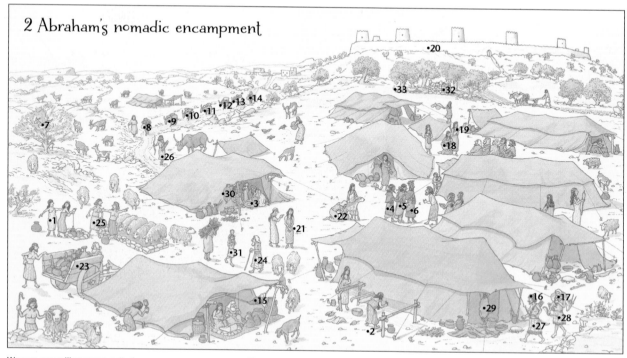

2 Abraham's nomadic encampment

Women quarrelling over a well 1
Spinner and weaver 2
Bread being baked on a stone 3
People in foreign dress 4 5 6
Goat stuck in a thorn bush 7
Donkeys in the caravan 8 9 10 11 12 13 14
Baby cradled in a hammock 15

Young men going hunting 16 17
Girl playing harp 18
Girl singing 19
Canaanite walled city 20
Servant girl being told off 21
Man milking a goat 22

Canaanite trading cart 23
Men wearing kilts in the same pattern 24 25 26 27 28
Goatskin wine containers 29 30
Boy carrying his little brother 31
Altar in a grove of trees 32
Fox 33

3 Slaves in Egypt

Men using a brick mould 1 2 3 4 5
Shaduf 6
Men carrying bundles of uncut straw 7 8 9
Slave-drivers whipping a slave 10 11
Ducks 12 13 14 15
Men gathering reeds 16
Woman coiling a basket from reeds 17
Boy trying to catch a lamb 18

Guards making sure the way ahead is clear 19 20 21 22
Girls dancing 23 24 25 26
Fleeing lions 27 28 29
Girls foraging 30 31 32
Frogs 33 34 35 36 37 38 39 40 41
Scribes at work 42 43
Cats 44 45 46 47 48
Barge with the princess on 49

Cattle 50 51 52 53 54 55 56 57 58
Silos 59 60 61 62
Children sharing a melon 63 64
Fox 65

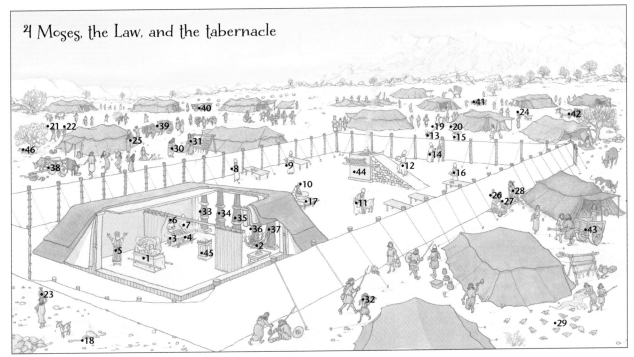

4 Moses, the Law, and the tabernacle

Ark of the covenant 1
Lamp stand with 7 branches 2
Priests laying loaves on a table 3 4
High priest 5
Priests 6 7 8 9 10 11 12 13 14 15 16
Bronze basin 17
Snake 18

Priests with silver trumpets 19 20
Men carrying a bunch of grapes 21 22
Women carrying water pots 23 24 25
Men fighting 26 27 28
Flock of quails 29
Women folding a length of cloth together 30 31
Child carrying his pet lamb on his shoulders 32

Pillars at the front of the tabernacle 33 34 35 36 37
Ox carts 38 39 40 41 42 43
Large altar 44
Small altar 45
Fox 46

5 Farming the land

Barley field being cut with a sickle 1
Sheaves of barley 2 3
Children riding on a threshing sledge 4 5 6
Woman winnowing 7
Vine-tenders 8 9
Children picking peas 10 11
Rock hyraxes 12 13
Hoes 14 15 16

Goat in an olive tree 17
Watchtowers 18 19 20
Tired farm worker having a rest 21
Midianite spies 22 23 24
Boy trying to run off with a loaf 25
Woman who has dropped her pot 26
Woman laying out figs 27
Woman watering a melon patch 28

Woman laying out flax 29
Fox 30

6 A battle against the Philistines

Goliath's sword, spear, and javelin 1 2 3
Goliath's feather-trimmed helmet 4
Baskets of food 5 6 7
Soldier sitting down 8
David flinging a stone with his sling 9
Goliath's shield-bearer running away 10
The royal suit of armour 11

Musician playing a harp 12
Stream running between the enemy camps 13
Soldiers roasting a lamb 14
Priest in the Israelite camp 15
Philistine supply carts 16 17 18 19 20 21 22
Philistine war chariots 23 24 25 26 27 28 29
Men with horn trumpets 30

King Saul 31
Vultures circling the battlefield 32 33 34 35 36
Blacksmith in the Philistine camp 37
Fox 38

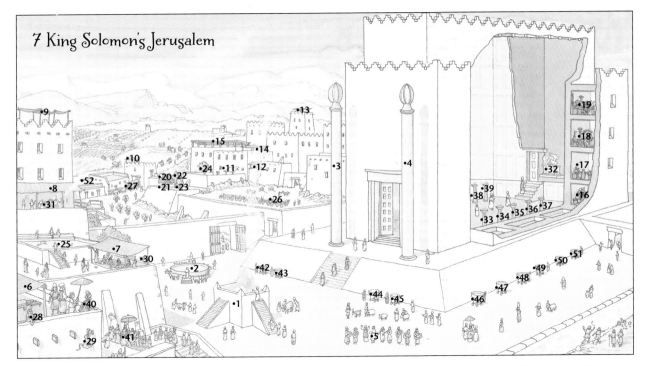

7 King Solomon's Jerusalem

Altar where sacrifices were burned   1
Huge bronze water tank   2
Jachin   3
Boaz   4
Band of musicians practising their instruments   5
Awnings providing rooftop shade   6 7 8 9 10 11 12 13
   14 15

Temple storerooms   16 17 18 19
Pomegranate trees   20 21 22 23 24
Palace children playing in an outdoor pool   25
Group of horse-drawn chariots   26
Wagon loaded with cedar trunks   27
Baboons   28 29 30
Cooks roasting a calf   31

Ark of the covenant   32
Gold lamp stands   33 34 35 36 37 38 39
King Solomon   40
Queen of Sheba   41
Washbasin carts   42 43 44 45 46 47 48 49 50 51
Fox 52

8 An Assyrian attack

Group of slingers   1
Battering rams   2 3
Blazing torches   4 5 6 7
Straw shields   8 9 10 11 12 13
Defeated fighter pleading for mercy   14
Carts   15 16
Assyrian emperor   17
People in a sword fight   18

Servants fanning the emperor   19 20
Ladders   21 22 23 24 25
Sheep   26 27
Goat   28
Assyrians falling off ladders   29 30
Children holding hands looking for parents   31 32
Children gathering figs for soldiers   33 34 35
Chariot being repaired   36

Laden camels bringing tribute   37
Woman carrying a child   38
Fox   39

9 Exiles in Babylon

Design on blue tiles on the Ishtar gate   1
Statue of Marduk   2
Different types of musical instruments   3 4 5
Slaves tending potted trees   6 7 8
Boat transporting a large tree   9
Boys fishing from coracles   10 11 12 13
Caged lion   14
Scribe recording the event on a wax tablet   15

Heron   16
Elephants   17 18
Archers guarding the procession   19 20 21 22
Ziggurat (stepped tower)   23
Group of Jews going out of the city by boat   24
Jews refusing to bow down to the Babylonian god   25 26 27
Parasols   28 29 30 31 32 33 34 35 36 37 38

Guard with a mastiff   39
Pickpocket in the crowd   40
Horse   41
Child eating dried dates   42
Fox   43

10 A census in Bethlehem

Couple pleading for a room   1
Roof shelters   2 3 4
Ox in a stable   5
Donkeys   6 7
King Herod's spies exchanging a secret note   8 9
Freedom fighter with a sword   10
Women carrying pots on their heads   11 12

African visitor   13
Roman soldiers   14 15 16 17 18
Shepherd boy trying to catch a runaway sheep   19
Goat eating a shoe   20
Family reunion   21
Young mother with her child   22
Local tax collector taking the census   23

Doves   24 25 26
Robber   27
Rabbi telling some Samaritans to find somewhere else to stay   28
Servant loading hay into a manger   29
Fox   30

11 A schoolboy in Nazareth

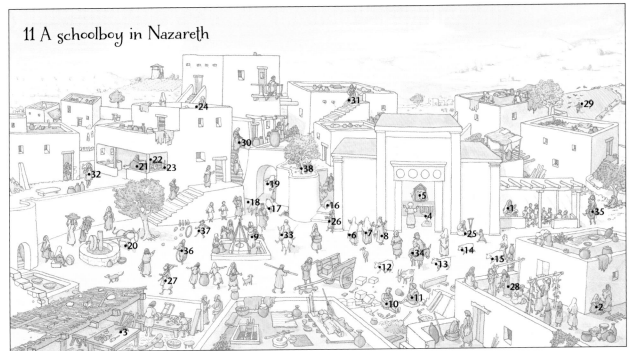

Rabbi teaching in the school room 1
Woman playing a harp 2
Bow drill 3
Menorah in the synagogue 4
Ark containing scrolls 5
Very religious men praying in the street 6 7 8
Mother drawing water from the well 9

Workers drinking from a wineskin 10 11
Sheep in the street 12 13 14 15 16 17 18 19
Donkey driving an olive mill 20
Oxen eating from a manger 21 22 23
Old man watching the world go by 24
Beggars with begging bowls 25 26 27
Village girls making a wedding canopy 28

Sower scattering seed from a basket 29
Women brushing out their houses 30 31
Shepherd carrying a lamb on his shoulders 32
People riding donkeys 33 34 35
Children playing 36 37
Fox 38

12 A fishing town on Lake Galilee

Queue of people waiting to pay the tax collector 1
Jesus preaching 2
Cattle drinking by the lake 3 4 5 6
People with crutches 7 8 9 10 11
Pair of boats with net hung between them 12
Baskets of fish 13 14 15 16 17 18
Woman trying to light her lamp from another's 19

Woman weaving at her loom 20
Man carrying a Roman soldier's pack 21
Children swimming in the lake 22 23 24 25 26 27
Man driving a team of oxen 28
Sandal seller 29
Olive oil seller 30
Cloth seller 31

Vegetable seller 32
Basket seller 33
Boys playing a board game in the sand 34
Man chasing a runaway donkey 35
Roman soldiers patrolling the lakeside 36 37
Fox 38

13 The Temple courtyard

Money changer 1
Lambs 2 3 4 5 6 7 8 9
Pigeon cage 10
Romans guarding the Temple 11 12 13 14 15 16
High priest 17
Priest directing the musicians 18
Pickpocket stealing money from a pilgrim 19
Musicians playing a psalm of worship 20

Pontius Pilate 21
Roof of the Temple sanctuary 22
Jesus pushing over a table and telling cheating traders to go 23
The Antonia fortress 24
Crane 25
Poor woman counting out coins 26
Someone chasing a dog 27

Judas Iscariot talking to some rabbis 28
Rabbi reading a scroll 29
Fox 30

14 The death of Jesus

Crucified criminals' bodies wrapped in cloth 1 2
Friends of Jesus carrying his body away 3
Stone tomb with a round stone door 4
Ravens 5 6 7
Olive trees near the site 8 9 10 11 12 13
Judas Iscariot 14
Pontius Pilate 15
Group of freedom fighters 16

Stray dogs 17 18
Crime notices 19 20 21
Beggars 22 23
Soldiers playing a dice game 24
Crown of thorns the executioners rammed on Jesus' head 25
Mallets 26 27
Man raking the sand 28

Top of the Temple building 29
Ladders 30 31
Shields 32 33 34 35 36 37 38 39 40
Someone planning mischief with his slingshot 41
John and Mary 42
Fox 43

15 Peter preaches about Jesus

Peter 1
Guards 2 3
Lady of the house 4
Oil lamps 5 6 7
Mosaic floor 8
Servants bringing plates of food 9 10
Cornelius 11
Donkey laden with goods 12

Rabbi 13
Scrolls in a cupboard 14
Child's ball 15
Iris in a vase 16
Mouse 17
Footstools 18 19 20
Cats 21 22
Sparrows 23 24

Slave with garden clippers 25
Children listening 26 27 28 29 30 31
Kitchen worker listening in 32
Slave taking notes on Peter's speech 33
Fox 34

16 Preaching in Corinth

Priscilla 1
Aquila 2
Soldiers inspecting the tent 3 4 5
Niches with statues 6 7 8
Amphorae (pottery storage jars) 9 10 11
Businessmen arguing 12 13
Silas 14
Timothy 15

Messenger racing through the marketplace 16
Carving of an emperor 17
Butcher's shop 18
Dog scavenging bones 19
Bread stall 20
Fruit stall 21
Storyteller surrounded by children 22
Shop where purple cloth is sold 23

Rich woman being carried through the streets 24
Funeral procession 25
Fox 26

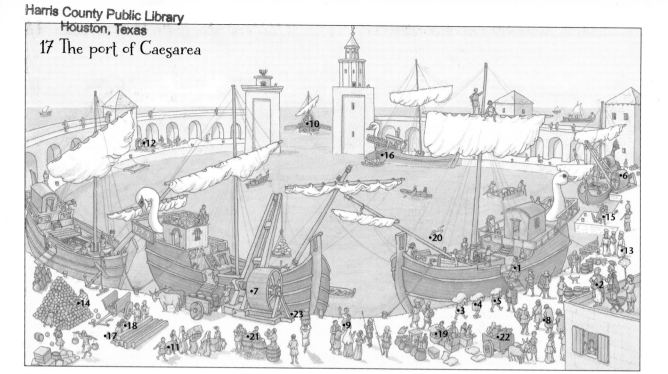

17 The port of Caesarea

Paul leaving for Rome 1
Festus watching Paul's departure 2
People carrying sacks of grain 3 4 5
Dockside cranes 6 7
Other prisoners being boarded onto the same ship as
  Paul 8
Local believers waving Paul farewell 9
Warship with many oars worked by galley slaves 10

Family struggling with luggage 11
Workmen mixing concrete for harbour repairs 12
Priests frowning at Paul being allowed to appeal their
  judgment 13
Children helping themselves to watermelons 14
Sailor lifting an anchor up 15
Steering oar being refitted 16
Men drinking wine who look like they've stolen it 17 18

Woman packing a hamper 19
Seagull swooping on someone's lunch 20
Man packing bottles into a barrel filled with straw 21
Wagon loaded with amphorae 22
Fox 23

Index

Numbers refer to spread numbers